www.capstonepub.com
Visit our website to find out more information about Heinemann-Raintree books.

To order:

☎ Phone 800-747-4992
🖥 Visit www.capstonepub.com to browse our catalog and order online.

Edited by Daniel Nunn, Rebecca Rissman, and Sian Smith
Designed by Cynthia Della-Rovere
Picture research by Mica Brancic
Production by Victoria Fitzgerald
Originated by Capstone Global Library Ltd
Printed and bound in China by South China Printing Company Ltd

16 15 14 13 12
10 9 8 7 6 5 4 3 2 1

Library of Congress Cataloging-in-Publication Data
Nunn, Daniel.
 Numbers in French: Les Chiffres / Daniel Nunn.
  p. cm.—(World languages - Numbers)
 Includes bibliographical references and index.
 ISBN 978-1-4329-6672-0—ISBN 978-1-4329-6679-9 (pbk.) 1. French language—Textbooks for foreign speakers—English—Juvenile literature. 2. Number concept—Juvenile literature. I. Title.
 PC2129.E5N87 2012
 448.2′421—dc23   2011050546

Acknowledgments
We would like to thank Shutterstock for permission to reproduce photographs: © Agorohov, © Aleksandrs Poliscuks, © Alex James Bramwell, © Andreas Gradin, © Andrey Armyagov, © archidea, © Arogant, © atoss, © Baloncici, © Benjamin Mercer, © blackpixel, © charles taylor, © Chris Bradshaw, © cloki, © dcwcreations, © DenisNata, © Diana Taliun, © Eric Isselée, © Erik Lam, © Fatseyeva, © Feng Yu, © g215, © Hywit Dimyadi, © Iv Nikolny, © J. Waldron, © jgl247, © joingate, © karam Miri, © Karkas, © kedrov, © LittleMiss, © Ljupco Smokovski, © Lori Sparkia, © Max Krasnov, © Michelangelus, © Mike Flippo, © mimo, © Nordling, © Olga Popova, © Pavel Sazonov, © pics fine, © Rosery, © Ruth Black, © Shmel, © Stacy Barnett, © Steve Collender, © Suzanna, © Tania Zbrodko, © topseller, © Vasina Natalia, © Veniamin Kraskov, © Vinicius Tupinamba, © Volodymyr Krasyuk, © Vorm in Beeld, © Winston Link, © xpixel.

Cover photographs reproduced with permission of Shutterstock: number 1 (© Leigh Prather), number 2 (© Glovatskiy), number 3 (© Phuriphat). Back cover photographs of toys of reproduced with permission of Shutterstock (© joingate, © Lori Sparkia, © Michelangelus, © Agorohov, © Tania Zbrodko).

We would like to thank Séverine Ribierre for her invaluable assistance in the preparation of this book.

Every effort has been made to contact copyright holders of material reproduced in this book. Any omissions will be rectified in subsequent printings if notice is given to the publisher.

Contents

Un

un chien

Il y a un chien.

Il y a un pull.

Deux

un chat

Il y a deux chats.

une chaussure

Il y a deux chaussures.

Trois

une fille

Il y a trois filles.

une chaise

Il y a trois chaises.

Quatre

un oiseau

Il y a quatre oiseaux.

un coussin

Il y a quatre coussins.

Cinq

un jouet

Il y a cinq jouets.

un livre

Il y a cinq livres.

Six

un manteau

Il y a six manteaux.

un crayon

Il y a six crayons.

Sept

une orange

Il y a sept oranges.

un biscuit

Il y a sept biscuits.

Huit

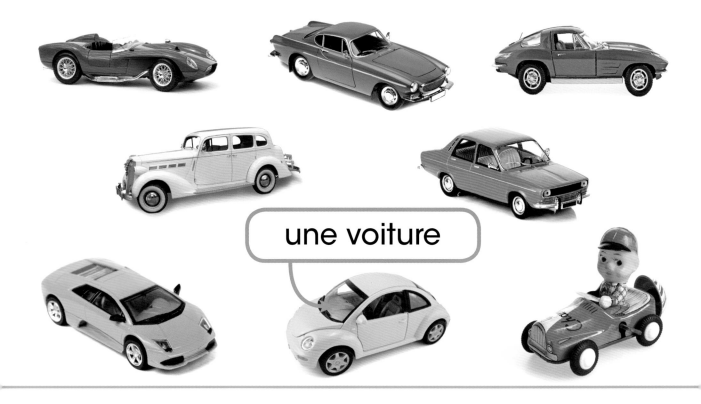

une voiture

Il y a huit voitures.

un chapeau

Il y a huit chapeaux.

Neuf

un ballon

Il y a neuf ballons.

une bougie

Il y a neuf bougies.

Dix

une pomme

Il y a dix pommes.

une fleur

Il y a dix fleurs.

Dictionary

French Word	How To Say It	English Word
ballon / ballons	bal-lon	balloon / balloons
biscuit / biscuits	bis-kwee	cookie / cookies
bougie / bougies	boo-gee	candle / candles
chaise / chaises	shez	chair / chairs
chapeau / chapeaux	sha-po	hat / hats
chat / chats	sha	cat / cats
chaussure / chaussures	sho-sur	shoe / shoes
chien	she-an	dog
cinq	sank	five
coussin / coussins	coo-san	cushion / cushions
crayon / crayons	kray-on	pencil / pencils
deux	duh	two
dix	deece	ten
fille / filles	feey	girl / girls
fleur / fleurs	flur	flower / flowers
huit	weet	eight

French Word	How To Say It	English Word
il y a	eel-ee-a	there is / there are
jouet / jouets	joo-ay	toy / toys
livre / livres	leevre	book / books
manteau / manteaux	man-toe	coat / coats
neuf	nuf	nine
oiseau / oiseaux	wa-zo	bird / birds
orange / oranges	or-onj	orange / oranges
pomme / pommes	pom	apple / apples
pull	pull	sweater
quatre	katre	four
sept	set	seven
six	seece	six
trois	trwa	three
un / une	un / oo-n	a
un / une	un / oo-n	one
voiture / voitures	vwa-ture	car / cars

Index

Notes for Parents and Teachers
In French, nouns are either masculine or feminine. The word for "a" or "one"
changes accordingly—either un (masculine) or une (feminine).